THE MIGHTY MISSISSIPPI FROM THE BLUFFS OF NATCHEZ

THE GATES OF DUNLEITH

NOLA NANCE OLIVER

Natchez

SYMBOL OF THE
OLD SOUTH

HASTINGS HOUSE · PUBLISHERS · NEW YORK

MONTEIGNE — Stairhall

This book is dedicated to Louise and Mary.

Foreword

Natchez derives its name from the sun-worshiping Indian tribe, the Natchez, who were the original owners of the area on which the city is located. It is situated in Adams county, in the southwestern part of the state of Mississippi, on bluffs 200 feet high overlooking the Mississippi River, and is midway between Memphis and New Orleans. It is accessible by railway, steamboat, motor highway and airway. It is particularly proud of the Natchez Trace Parkway, a modern concrete road-over an old Indian trace or trail from Nashville to Natchez. This highway is a link in one of the most important commercial and historic highways in the United States reaching from Washington, D. C., to Mexico.

Today Natchez is a recognized center of interest because in the city and its vicinity there are a greater number of original ante-bellum mansions than in any other community in America — some 75 or more.

Natchez is the second oldest town in the United States, being next in age to St. Augustine, Florida. It has lived under five different flags, each of which contributed romantic flavor to the section. From 1714 to 1763 it was under the flag of France; from 1764 to 1780 under the flag of England; and from 1780 to 1798 under the flag of Spain. In 1798 the first United States flag in the Lower Mississippi Valley was raised in Natchez. Years after the raising of the "stars and stripes", another flag which some call "the conquered banner", the beloved flag of the Confederate States of America, floated over Natchez, 1861-'65.

Natchez "Under the Hill" applies to that part of the town along the water front and under the bluffs. It flourished during the heyday of steamboating on the Mississippi. The inroads of the river have washed away the streets, and only a few buildings remain. One very interesting home, "Magnolia Vale", has been preserved and is presented in this book.

The majority of these old homes contain original pieces of furniture, china, coin silver service, draperies, carpets, wall decorations of exquisite workmanship, huge mirrors in massive goldleaf frames, paintings bearing authentic signatures of great masters, and hand-carved marble mantels. Laces, silks, and rich costumes are displayed today by third, fourth and fifth generations.

It seems hardly possible that the world could move on and leave one small community undisturbed in its ancient grandeur. The hand of destiny seems indeed to uphold and enshrine this hallowed region. The estates have descended from generation to generation, many of them today being owned and occupied by descendants of the original owners.

Natchezians have been entirely satisfied, even proud, to be termed "provincial". A sense of inherent aristocracy has given these people a secure and placid self-sufficiency which neither time nor stress of outside conditions nor the frettings of progress can jar or mar.

Within the past ten years tourists have come. They clamored for entertainment. And now, maintaining the established reputation for "hospitality of the true South", each Spring season Natchez opens wide her gates and invites the world to come "where the Old South still lives".

The "company dress" of great-grandparents, which has been sacredly stored away for scores of years, is brought out, and overnight the whole town, in manners and dress, returns to those halcyon days of long ago. The streets are filled with young and old in ante-bellum costumes. Sweet olive trees and magnolia trees are in fragrant bloom, flower gardens are fresh and inviting, moss-draped oaks ring with the song of native birds, the old homes are opened, treasures are placed on view, and visitors are given a Southland welcome. The "Pilgrimage" is on!

In addition to guided tours through ante-bellum houses special entertainments are planned for each evening. Confederate balls, historical pageants, and many other colorful events of the past are re-enacted. Spirituals are sung in old-fashioned Negro churches where the "pahson" is eager to greet "our white friends". On spacious plantation grounds an old-time Southern barbecue prepared by black mammies will be served.

A custom which has long prevailed in Natchez is the placing of coins in a box for old darky beggars. On Saturdays every merchant observes "Penny Day", as it is called. It originated as a time saver, the box being placed in a convenient location to avoid interruption of the store's business. There are many regular "customers" for this feature and they are always welcome. "Penny Day" is a thoughtful, good-natured gesture to the needy Negro from his "white folks".

Pictures of the old homes with accurate data and intimate stories and legends constitute *Natchez, Symbol of the Old South*. Most of the photographs are by Earl Norman.

A fascinating visit is given you by one who knows and loves the Southland. You will be delighted and enriched.

UNCLE WASH, A REGULAR
CUSTOMER ON PENNY DAY

The Natchez Tribe

A bronze plaque of a handsome Indian chief has been erected in a granite wall overlooking the great "Father of Waters", in memory of the Natchez Indian tribe from which the city of Natchez derives its name.

The Natchez Indians were of Aztec origin and were in possession of the Natchez country when the French came in 1700. They were sun-worshiping Indians, and their great chief proclaimed himself "brother to the Sun".

White Apple village, ten miles south of Natchez, was headquarters of the Natchez tribe. They resented the invasion of the French explorers into their country, and because of an insult (real or fancied) to their Chief by a French Commandant, on November 28, 1729, the Indians slaughtered the entire French settlement at Fort Rosalie. Later a French colony, with the assistance of the Choctaws, a warring Indian tribe, annihilated every member of the Natchez tribe.

Undoubtedly this was the country of the Natchez tribe, and the beautiful plaque is a deserved reminder of the days when the land was one hundred per cent American.

ON NATCHEZ TRACE

Natchez Trace

Opportunity for easy travel, over trails that were once Indian foot paths, is offered now to motorists on perfect concrete highways. Modern roads, which slowly evolved from dirt roads to paved highways, stretch from Nashville, Tennessee, in a continuous smooth concrete ribbon to Natchez, on the great Mississippi River.

Days when the beauty of the Southland could be viewed only from a steamboat deck; days when transportation of passenger and freight could be handled only by oxcart or slow stage coach or horse and buggy (a three-weeks journey from Nashville to Natchez) are gone forever, and soon the Deep South will be directly connected by a day's pleasant journey with all the cities and towns along the Natchez Trace.

By treaty with Choctaw and Chickasaw Indian tribes the United States Government in 1801 secured a permit to open the Natchez Trace as a wagon road over which the mails could travel.

That same trail or "trace" from Nashville to Natchez is 500 miles of consecutive beauty spots along continuous acres of parkways and historic highways.

Mrs. Roan Fleming Byrnes, serving as President of the Natchez Trace Highway Committee, in a recent publication says:

"The ancient trail was traveled by most of the well-known figures in the history of our country: Jefferson Davis; Peggy and Lorenzo Dow, the revivalists; the fast riding John Morgan; the famous Audubon. Lafayette rode over the Trace during his visit to the Natchez country; Aaron Burr was given his preliminary trial for treason under two liveoaks just beside the Trace; Meriwether Lewis died at an inn on the Trace when returning from his Western explorations.

"The life of Andrew Jackson is closely interwoven with the windings of the Natchez Trace. At Springfield plantation, in Jefferson county, Mississippi, Jackson was married to Rachael Robards; and, near Nashville, Tennessee, is the 'Hermitage', the home he built for Rachael.

"It was when marching his rejected Tennessee militia homeward over the Trace from Natchez to Nashville in 1813 that Jackson acquired his famous nickname, 'Old Hickory'."

The unusual beauty of the deep cut roadways, worn down by travel throughout the years, and the overlapping, moss-draped trees, will be preserved as far as possible.

Many of these old roads running into Natchez lead through deep, tunnel-like ways whose sides are sheer walls ten to eighty feet high and draped with long fronds of overhanging Spanish moss.

These roadways of tunnels and curves are weird and beautiful, affording an irresistible attraction for all travelers.

Airlie

Built prior to 1790, "Airlie" is a rambling, wide-spread building of cottage type, on a rolling elevation at the end of Myrtle street. It attracts attention through its unusual simplicity of exterior. Its architecture is entirely different from other ante-bellum homes in the community.

This great departure from the usual style is due to the age of Airlie. Its original building date is ahead of all the available history of Natchez.

Additions have been made, from time to time, until today Airlie stands twelve rooms broad, reaching a row of venerable cedars with their swaying moss which sweeps the eaves of this old home of the Ayres P. Merrill family.

The central portion is built on old Spanish style, with beams and timbers held together by wooden pegs; later additions show that these were made by somewhat improved methods.

Airlie is often referred to as "the old Buckner home". It was occupied by the Buckner family at the time of its first recorded history and during the War Between the States when conflicts at Airlie left blood stains on its floors and walls which are clearly visible today.

This house was for a time used as a hospital for Northern soldiers.

When Airlie passed from the Buckner family it became the property of another family of distinction, that of Ayres P. Merrill. whose descendants occupy Airlie today, with its treasure of rosewood and mahogany antiques.

The present Merrill family are the proud possessors of hundreds of pieces of Du Barry and other imported china from France and Belgium, as well as a silver service of rare design and sacred antiquity which might well excite the envy of Royalty itself.

There are many persons who believe Airlie was the first residence built in the Natchez territory. No definite date in authentic records can be found.

Arlington

Where Natchez' Main street ends, the great wide gates of Arlington open. Live oaks with pendant gray moss line the driveway, which winds through beds of vari-colored irises to one of the most distinctively attractive ante-bellum homes in the South.

Of Southern Colonial type, constructed of red brick with stately white Tuscan columns supporting the upper story gallery, Arlington today, more than a century old, presents a magnificent appearance.

The great carved entrance door leading to the spacious hall is crowned with intricately wrought fanlights, and the broad veranda is approached by wide steps of concrete.

Arlington was built for Mrs. Jane White, eldest daughter of Pierre Surget, who came from France in the early days of Natchez. The house was completed about 1820 but on the very first night of her residence in the home of her heart's desire Mrs. White passed away suddenly. Many tales have been told of a mysterious death but none has been verified. At her death Mrs. White left Arlington and all its treasures to her sister, Mrs. Bingaman.

IMPOSING COLUMNED DOORWAY LEADING FROM HALL *(opposite)*

Five generations of the Pierre Surget family occupied Arlington. Each in turn contributed to its wealth of rare treasures. The original furniture was imported from France.

Across the broad hallway which is hung with rare paintings by old-world masters such as Vernet, Baroccio, Carlo Lolci, and Coccanari, is the Music Room which contains a spinet more than three hundred years old. There are family portraits in this room — some of musicians in the family — by such renowned artists as Sully, Audubon, Albani, Fidauza, and Maratti.

The Library holds some five thousand books.

Mrs. Hubert Barnum, the present owner of Arlington, comes from a long line of Natchez aristocracy. Arlington was given her as a wedding gift from her husband, who recently passed away. Mrs. Barnum while keeping the home atmosphere of Arlington has made it, also, a veritable private museum, rich in beauty, in rare books, and antiques.

Auburn

Built in 1812, a full century and a quarter ago, by Dr. Stephen Duncan, "Auburn" mansion is noted today as in bygone historic days for its architectural beauty and the natural beauty of its surrounding acres.

Auburn is a magnificent red brick structure with great white columns supporting its broad front galleries. The bricks were made on the premises by slave labor. On the first floor are spacious drawing rooms, a large dining room, a family dining room, library, smoking room, and two hallways. Above stairs are six huge bedrooms with high ceilings.

In the rear of the main mansion is a two-storied brick kitchen which is connected with the main building by a flagged patio. The servants' quarters are above with the kitchen and pantries on the ground floor. The kitchen has the giant fireplace with cranes and pots and the old-time "spit" where meats were roasted.

Entrance to Auburn is through a classic doorway which has been aptly called "an architect's dream of beauty".

CLASSIC
ENTRANCE
DOORWAY

Inside the house there is a majestic spiral stairway rising to the grand high hallway, without support except at its base. This amazing feature intrigues the imagination.

In early days Auburn entertained many celebrities, among them Henry Clay, Edward Everett Hale, and John Howard Payne. The same gracious hospitality maintains today.

Auburn is the property of the city of Natchez by deed of gift from Stephen Duncan, and is used as the deed stipulates for the "amusement, entertainment, and recreation, without cost or monetary consideration, of Natchez citizens". It is the handsome headquarters of several distinguished local clubs.

The women's clubs of Natchez have undertaken the task of furnishing the lower floor with valuable antiques of the period of its original furnishings.

The acreage surrounding it is known as Duncan Park in compliment to the Duncan family who gave it to the city. It contains huge, aged, moss-draped oaks, alluring sweet olive trees, famous magnolias, shrubbery and vines, old-fashioned gardens, a golf course, and playground with swings and merry-go-rounds used every day in the year for the health and frolic of children.

The Unsupported Spiral Stairway Rises to the Grand Hallway.
(opposite)

Old Milk House. Slaves pumped cool cistern water into long zinc vats providing Auburn's cooling system for its crocks of milk.

Food prepared in the kitchen below the servants' quarters was carried in hot urns to dining rooms by servants stationed along "the ways".

Belmont

Sturdy as the Rock of Gibraltar stands this imposing Neo-Greek mansion. It was known originally as "Cleremont", and was built in the early 40's by one Loxley Thistle.

Storm and strife have beaten against the doors of this stronghold but it was built after a disastrous tornado which put a great fear in the minds of builders of that period, and Belmont (as it was renamed) was constructed to resist fierce storms, although at the same time exquisite lines of beauty were maintained.

This place with its thirty acres of land has changed hands oftener than any ante-bellum home in Natchez. Its history is broken and uncertain. It was undoubtedly built by imported craftsmen who had the help of local carpenters and slave labor.

Many prominent families of Natchez are identified with Belmont at some period in its history. Within its fort-like walls Natchez elite often sipped rare old wine from its private sub-cellar in frequent celebrations.

Belmont has its ghost story of whispering souls wandering through the high-ceilinged halls — ghosts created to scare the slaves, and "whispers" which proved to be the swishing of chimney swallows rushing in and out of their nests.

The approach to Belmont is a majestic line of moss-draped cedars and giant oak trees standing sentinel-like over the gardens of days long passed.

Louis Fry, present owner, plans the complete restoration of Belmont. It may soon ring with echoes of happier days.

Belvidere

On Homochitto street, in the shadow of magnificent "Dunleith", is a simple white cottage, "Belvidere", which for generations has been the home of the Henderson family.

Originally Belvidere was the center of a fourteen acre tract of wooded land which was the property of Christopher Miller, who was secretary to the Spanish Governor of Natchez, Gayoso de Lemos. The Hendersons are descendants of Christopher Miller.

Simple and unostentatious this small cottage stands with her very toes, as it were, on the street where once broad acreage spread. These acres gave space in later years for a public school and a paved highway.

Belvidere is more than 100 years old, and has been for more than a century owned and occupied by one family.

It is simply furnished, and much of it is the original furniture, more than 100 years old. Two pictures of special interest adorn the walls, silhouettes of Samuel Brooks and his wife — "the first Mayor of Natchez and his Lady". These pictures were made in 1753.

Rare Venetian glass and china and many exquisite pieces of porcelain are found in Belvidere.

The property is now owned and occupied by Mrs. Florence Henderson Kelly and her son and daughter, Thomas G. and Ellen N.

Brandon Hall

This old home is not in the immediate Natchez area but its owner and his descendants are so closely allied with all that is Natchez that Brandon Hall is rightfully considered a Natchez asset and is included in its list of ante-bellum homes.

Gerard Brandon of Ireland came to Natchez prior to the Revolutionary War, and more than a century ago "Selma Plantation", from whose acres came the grounds of Brandon Hall, was built by him. Mr. Brandon was a successful farmer and was one of the original pecan growers in the county. He came to Natchez from South Carolina.

Brandon Hall was built by Gerard Brandon the Third in 1856, and stands today a splendid monument to a grand old family. It is sturdily constructed. Its timbers are secured with thumb screws and wooden pegs.

Cherry Grove

Built of primeval timbers, cut and hewn by slaves on the place, the old home at Cherry Grove plantation "sits tight" secured by dependable wooden pegs. It was built in 1788 when time and expense of labor were of little consideration, and nails and modern building equipment were not available.

Pierre Surget of La Rochelle, France, built this Spanish style house, on a Spanish land grant, for his wife, Katherine d'Hubert, and from this couple have come some of Natchez' most prominent families.

Mr. Surget was a seaman for many years before coming to the Natchez country, and Cherry Grove was built with the sturdiness of a seaworthy vessel.

The home has never passed out of the Surget family. Its present owner, Mrs. Carlotta Surget McKittrick, now possesses the original Spanish land grant made to Pierre Surget in the 1700's.

In a small cemetery within sight of the old home, enclosed by an imported iron fence, lie the bodies of Pierre Surget and his wife, Katherine.

Descendants of the Surget slaves remain in the "quarters" to look after the place, and to plant and gather cotton from its vast acres.

The house is unoccupied. Much of the original furnishing remains intact, and a Surget heir is today sole owner of the quaint old dwelling of her illustrious forbears.

VARINA HOWELL AND JEFFERSON DAVIS WERE MARRIED IN THIS ROOM.

The Briers

Could Jefferson Davis and his beloved wife, Varina, return to The Briers today they would be pleased to find it in a perfect state of preservation.

"The Briers", a typical story-and-a-half country home, was given to Louise Kemp at the time of her marriage to William Burr Howell, who was a cousin of Aaron Burr. And here Varina Howell was born May 7, 1826. This home was the scene of Varina's marriage to Jefferson Davis on February 12, 1845. Mr. Davis later became "President of the Confederacy".

The house is situated on a knoll overlooking the Mississippi river, with a view of the cotton lands of Louisiana. The view of the Mississippi shown in the end papers was taken from the lawn of this house. It stands in the center of a forest of oak, pine, and pecan trees, and can be reached by only one narrow winding roadway, through deep woods, around bayous and ravines, hanging heavy with bushes and brambles. The house is quite similar to the Virginia type of country home.

When the present owner, Mrs. W. W. Wall, purchased The Briers a few years ago, it was in a sad state of dilapidation. By great and loving labor, and generous expenditure of money and time, The Briers today is in perfect condition. It is now a charming credit to Natchez and to the memory of Jefferson Davis and his wife, Varina.

The early architectural lines have been followed and materials similar to the original ones have been used. The broad veranda across the entire front, with many small wooden pillars and hand-turned spindle bannisters, the wide entrance steps, the quaint old dormer windows with their 12-pane sashes and heavy green blinds, form the perfect picture of the original plantation home of the Howells and Jefferson Davis.

The simplicity of the floor plan is pleasing. The furniture includes many reproductions of rare original pieces. There is a restful, sacred serenity in The Briers worthy of its illustrious original owners.

For the pleasure of visitors from the outside world, the present mistress keeps open house throughout the year, and hundreds of interested persons from every part of the United States pass through the portals of this home—the shrine of Jefferson Davis and Varina Howell.

The Burn

Another old home that was once situated in the center of vast acreage is "The Burn". Streets have been cut through, lots sold and residences erected until today this quaint old home, originally the residence of John P. Walworth of Ohio, is in the very heart of the residence district of Natchez.

While the "old Walworth home", as it was so long known, was built about 1834, its most interesting history is concerned with the war of 1861-65.

The Burn is a homey-looking house of the story-and-a-half cottage type with spacious halls and nineteen rooms in the main building. High ceilings, mahogany woodwork, and wide, hand-rubbed board floors are indicative of its early period.

By reason of its spacious and numerous rooms, and its accessibility to the river front and the Battery, "The Burn" was made headquarters for the Federal Artillery in the War Between the States. With only 24 hours' notice the family left their comfortable home to be occupied by the enemy. Major Coleman and his soldiers took possession of The Burn, and today on a window pane in the house can be seen the Major's full name as cut there by a diamond more than seventy-five years ago.

Within the last few years The Burn has been purchased by S. B. Laub, who is a direct descendant of the Beekman family. Mr. and Mrs. Laub have reclaimed and rebuilt every part of the old house with strict observance of the original architecture.

AN
INTERESTING
TREATMENT
OF
TRANSOM
AND
SIDE LIGHTS

26

A letter from the granddaughter of the original owner of The Burn written to its present owners and published in the *Natchez Democrat* tells the complete story:

"The Burn property when purchased by John P. Walworth in 1834 extended from Union street to Clifton Heights. The home was erected the same year, and got its name from the Scotch, meaning 'The Brook', which ran through the property where Pearl street now is.

"Architects and builders were brought from the East, the finest that could be found. It took more than a year to build, and has been compared to the Temple, for scarcely the sound of hammer was heard in its erection. The grand old home has stood fire, storm, and war.

"When Grant's army took possession of the town, The Burn became army headquarters, and was later turned into a hospital for Union soldiers. The wonderful old trees, the lawn and gardens fell before the axe and sword.

"After war clouds rolled away it was restored to its owner in a ruined condition. Generations have passed over its threshold loving it as a living being. The sons of the family bravely answered their country's call to arms and returned with untarnished records. Many brides have left its loving care. The mystery of life, birth and death have hallowed its walls with pride and sorrow.

"We relinquish our ownership rights into other hands; our escutcheon unsullied by debt or shame.

"We rejoice that it will be again a loved home, and may the happiness of the Walworth name continue to follow and bless the present owners."

Choctaw

Such dilapidated grandeur cannot be found in all the country around as one beholds at Choctaw. "Built to endure and determined not to fall" seems to ring from every stone and pillar of this gigantic old mansion. Once it was the center of a city block but now on the busy corner of Wall and High streets traffic of every sort brushes its very door.

Because this property was so long owned and occupied by a Natchez philanthropist, Alvarez Fisk, "Choctaw" is known far and wide as the "old Fisk home".

This stately example of classic architecture was built by one Sarah Neibert. Records show that it was deeded to Alvarez Fisk about 1840. Fisk was born in Massachusetts in 1783. During the early 90's Choctaw was used as "Stanton College for Women", and many Natchez women were educated there.

Time and decay have had their turn at Choctaw. The great stone pillars stand proudly, and boldly present a magnificent front; exquisite fanlights adorn the great doors which were built extra wide to accommodate the hoopskirted ladies of early days; walls and lofty ceilings stand in sturdy defiance of wind and rain and vandalism, and yet the crumbling corners, the tumbling formal entrance, and the rundown appearance of Choctaw produce a feeling of solemn sadness.

The foundation and walls of Choctaw are firm, and the day may come when this old palace will be restored to its former beauty and glory.

Concord

"Concord" was built in 1788 by Don Gayoso de Lemos, representative in the Natchez Territory of the King of Spain.

The name, "Concord", was chosen because the Governor felt that this word expressed the status of his people living in peace and amity.

The dwelling was two-and-a-half stories. The lower floor was of brick and the upper portion was frame. There was a driveway beneath the long flight of steps at the front entrance. The house was richly furnished with importations from Spain.

A few years ago "Concord" was destroyed by fire and Natchez lost an intriguing landmark.

Today the handsome iron-railed outside double stairway marks the spot that was once the ruling center of government, and the social hub during the colorful days of the Spanish regime.

COTTAGE GARDENS—STAIR HALL

Cottage Gardens

When "Cottage Gardens" was built, some hundred and forty years ago, Natchez was young, and homes at that time were of compact, inconspicuous design.

The land upon which this home stands was a part of the original Spanish grant to Don Jose Vidal, a young Spanish nobleman. "Cottage Gardens" was so named because of the beautiful gardens surrounding the cottage. It is recorded that these gardens were destroyed during the War Between the States when Union soldiers used the grounds as a pasture for their horses.

Don Jose Vidal was a military governor and Captain in a Spanish army. His duties took him across the river from Natchez to a place now known as Vidalia. When his beloved young wife died her tomb was built on a high bluff on the estate overlooking the Mississippi River. While engaged in official service across the broad waters, Capt. Vidal could look out at any moment and see the spot where his beautiful Donna Vidal was buried. Don Jose is buried in a Natchez Cemetery. A great shaft has been erected above his grave and is inscribed with a lengthy epitaph which mentions that "he was a friend of his Sovereign".

LIVING ROOM AND DINING ROOM

Cottage Gardens has been for several generations owned and occupied by the Foster family. Although the exterior is on simple lines, the house is surprisingly spacious. The wide hall through the center contains a stairway of unusual architectural attractiveness. Its broad steps with mahogany handrailing lead up along the left wall almost to the ceiling, then leaving the wall the stairway crosses the hall in a graceful spiral curve and the ascending flight is finished along the right wall.

At the rear end of the hall is a beautiful arched doorway with fanlight above and plain side glass. It is a facsimile of the entrance door at the opposite end of the hall.

From the present owners, the Foster family, comes Mary Kate Norman, the wife of Earl Norman, whose photographic art in picturing the old homes of Natchez has given him a prominent place among artists of the South.

THIS FAMILY ROOM IN
COTTAGE GARDENS HAS AN
EIGHT FOOT BED AND A CHILD'S BED.

THE TOMB OF
DON JOSE VIDAL

D'Evereux

By recent engineering survey Highway No. 61 from Memphis to New Orleans passes the grounds that once formed a part of D'Evereux acres. Motorists on this highway, when within a mile of Natchez, can see this mansion, in perfect architecture, standing like a great Greek temple near the roadway. Sweeping tropical moss hangs from the sentinel oaks which guard this magnificent home.

Built in 1840 for William St. John Elliott and his wife, it was given her family name, "D'Evereux", and this home, one of the most spacious in the community, was the scene of many happy affairs for the socially prominent.

Great double drawing rooms and a banquet room, while not containing the original furnishings, show woodwork and walls, hand-turned railings and doorways, evidence of the excellent taste of the builders.

After more than forty years the master-owner of D'Evereux died. The home was closed for a long while; later the widow with some of her young relatives opened the mansion and it became again the scene of many joyful gatherings.

Upon the death of Mrs. Elliott, "D'Evereux" was willed to her niece, Mrs. Margaret Martin Shields. During Mrs. Shields' occupancy, it was selected as the most perfect home, in style and setting, in the entire Southland, and for this reason it is shown in that exquisite motion picture, "The Heart of Maryland".

Within the past few years D'Evereux has been purchased by Miss Myra Smith of Chicago. With great pride in the ownership of one of the South's most majestic ante-bellum homes, Miss Smith has restored every portion of the old home, which today presents such magnificent perfection as to bring forth exclamations of wonder from all who travel that section of the Natchez Trace highway.

Cherokee

One of the most attractive of Natchez' ante-bellum houses is the recently reclaimed Cherokee, built in 1794 by Jesse Greenfield on land acquired under Spanish grant.

In 1810 David Michie purchased the property and added the classic front. The present owner, Mr. Charles Byrnes, has reclaimed the old Irish Manor House and its grounds, using wherever possible the style and materials of the original.

Cherokee stands on a great elevation overlooking Natchez. It is across the street from Choctaw and within calling distance of Connelly's Tavern on Ellicott Hill.

Dunleith

This house, built in 1849 by Gen. Dahlgreen, is situated in perfectly kept terraced grounds, surrounded by symetrically planted oak trees which have grown to giant size. A long driveway from the tall iron gate at the street entrance to the porch steps bring one to "Dunleith", a veritable Greek temple.

Dunleith is almost one hundred years old. The land on which it stands is part of a Spanish grant of 700 acres, and was the site of the original home which was destroyed by fire (caused by lightning) in 1845. In the rear of the present Dunleith are the stables which belonged to the original house.

At the death of Leslie Carpenter a few years ago this property was inherited by his widow and her son, J. N. Carpenter. No more perfect example of a Colonial mansion of the Old South can be found. The house and grounds are under the constant care of scientific gardeners and caretakers.

The story of Dunleith is incomplete until its legend has been told:

> "At the court of Louis Philippe, last King of France, a lady in waiting was Miss Isabel Percy, who visited Dunleith to try to forget a terrible heart hurt. She played the harp, and sang in a beautiful voice. At evening, just at dusk, her sweet mournful songs can still be heard in the parlors of Dunleith. When twilight turns to darkness, the swish of her silken skirts can be heard as she ascends the broad stairway to her private rooms above."

I know not how true this tale may be,
I tell it as 'twas told to me.

Edgewood

Edgewood, erected in 1855, shared with "Mount Repose" the distinction of being a part of the original Bisland estate. It is a simple plantation home, located on the Pine Ridge road, and is today occupied by direct descendants of the original owner, who maintain the estate as nearly as possible in accord with the original plans.

Situated on rolling greensward with a declivity at the rear, the house is two stories in front and three in the back. Straight, square lines are observed in its architecture. A porch extends across the entire front supported by double white columns. The outlook is into a group of restful, moss-covered oaks in the midst of which is a natural pond.

Edgewood is the home of Mr. and Mrs. S. H. Lamden, who with their young sons, S. H. III and Waldo, occupy this home of their forefathers. It is kept, from day to day, in the same style of ante-bellum home as in days gone by.

Many descendants of the original slaves of the Lamdens live today in the "quarters" on the place.

From "Beaupres" and other old plantations have come many possessions of rarest antiquity to Edgewood. There are portraits by the famous artist James Reed Lamden; among these is an exquisite portrait of his mother, who was Prudence Harrison; another is of Dr. John Flavel Carmichael, a member of the original staff of George Washington, painted by Gilbert Stuart.

Furnishings at Edgewood are of soft tones in rosewood and mahogany. Drawing rooms, dining room, and bed rooms are filled with valuable antiques — all in daily use by the present family. Edgewood retains today all the charm and beauty that it had nearly a hundred years ago.

Elgin

The history of "Elgin" dates from about 1838 when it was owned by the Dunbar family, and was named Elgin for the Dunbar estate in Scotland.

It is about eight miles from Natchez, and for many years was the home of the Jenkins family, whose descendants are prominent citizens of Natchez. Mr. Jenkins was a member of the Academy of Natural Science, and gave much time and scientific attention to the grounds of Elgin.

The old-fashioned frame building with spacious halls and wide galleries stands on a knoll in a broad clearing surrounded by a forest of oaks and pecans.

In 1914 Capt. Jenkins sold Elgin to the late Thornton Green of Michigan. Prior to that transfer "Elgin" while changing owners, each time was bought by descendants of its original owner.

Elgin was far-famed for its gardens and orchards, traces of which remain today and are being reclaimed by the latest purchasers of the property, Mr. and Mrs. W. S. R. Beane of New York and Natchez. The Beanes will make "Elgin" their permanent home.

Elms

Amid great elm trees and sturdy liveoaks is a wide, rambling house, its galleries bannistered with graceful iron grill encircling three sides of the structure. This is "Elms". It is the home of Mr. and Mrs. Joseph Kellogg. It is a close neighbor of the "Greenleaves" estate.

Elms was for a long time known as "the old Drake home". Its intricate rambling porticos, unusual stairway, and beautiful gardens came to the Kelloggs by fortunate inheritance. Mrs. Kellogg is a direct descendant of the Drake family. Benjamin Drake was president of Elizabeth College, which has the distinction of being the first college in the United States to permit the teaching of branches of higher education to women.

With the home and its acres of lovely gardens Mrs. Kellogg inherited a house filled with rare antique rosewood furniture.

The main building of Elms, a two-and-a-half-story structure, was built in the late 1700's. The exact date is not disclosed by available old records. As the property passed from descendant to descendant rooms have been added.

A striking feature of the house is a lacy wrought-iron stairway unlike any other in all America and believed to have been imported from Portugal. The stairway is built in a corridor, and is in harmony with the generous display of dainty, hand-turned work around the outer galleries.

Ceilings are low and give Spanish atmosphere to the architecture.

A series of old call bells, each with a different tone to indicate the location, are still in use in the various rooms.

The famous gardens in the rear have been reclaimed by the present mistress of Elms. Winding walks lead along flower beds of old-fashioned petunias, brilliant verbenas, phlox, roses and azaleas, edged with prim cut boxwood, while giant yuccas stand stiff as formal guards with white plumed headdress.

A great part of the original Elms estate has been sold, and today one of Natchez' modern school buildings stands across the street, giving the children of this school a daily picture lesson of home and life of the proud Old South.

Ellicott Hill

Artists and architects from far and near come to see the quaint old house, known as "Connelly's Tavern", on Ellicott Hill. It is a sturdy, perfectly proportioned old house, built of brick and wood, its timbers said to have come from abandoned sailing vessels.

The style of architecture is early Spanish. It stands on a high elevation, overlooking with aristocratic disdain the industrial enterprises which have come in during the years to supplant the once exclusive neighborhood of its original outlook. In early days, about the end of the Civil War, the place was known as "Gilreath's Hill".

The tavern was built in 1795. It has been occupied by many distinguished families.

The records show that at one time it was the home of "The Natchez High School". It was so used just after the War Between the States, when it was purchased by Wilson R. Gilreath.

Within the last few years the old building has commanded the greatest degree of public interest. Its historic value is unmatched. In addition to serving as the abode of many celebrated men, it attained fame as Connelly's Tavern when Aaron Burr and Blennerhasset met therein for secret conferences.

The most outstanding historic fact of the old Hill, itself, is that it is the spot whereon Col. Andrew Ellicott raised the first United States flag in February 1797 over the District of Natchez. Since that episode the spot has been known as "Ellicott Hill".

Dilapidation followed the wake of time. However, so sturdy were its timbers and so solid its foundation, it was possible to restore the old building on the hill.

The work of restoration has been accomplished by the Natchez Garden Club. Every old line has been carefully retained. Concrete floors of the kitchen and Tap Room, plastered walls, cypress grill work, solid doors, and roof are exact replicas of the originals. The old retaining walls and moats of brick have been replaced as originally at great cost. Today Ellicott Hill is shining in the full resplendency of its original glory. It is the present home of the Natchez Garden Club.

FIREPLACE IN OLD TAVERN ROOM AT CONNELLY'S TAVERN

Elmscourt

A short drive from Natchez, over a modern highway which was originally an Indian trail, through iron gates into a virgin forest, brings one a first glimpse of Elmscourt.

This mansion was erected about the year 1810 by Louis Evans, who was the first Sheriff of Adams county. He occupied it until 1851, at which time Frank Surget bought it for his daughter Jane as a gift when she married Ayers P. Merrill. It is said that Frank Surget was one of the three multi-millionaires in the United States at that time.

Jane and her husband opened wide the doors of their palatial home. General U. S. Grant was a frequent guest of Elmscourt, and by reason of this friendly contact, Ayres Merrill was appointed Minister to Belgium when Grant became President.

Elmscourt was originally Colonial in architecture but to please his wife Mr. Merrill changed it into an Italian Renaissance villa. The exquisite lacy iron work around its long galleries was imported from Belgium.

The dainty antique furnishings in parlors, library, and dining room are in perfect harmony with this period of architecture. Many original pieces are retained. At the death of Ayres P. Merrill "Elmscourt" descended to his son, Ayres P. Merrill Jr., and was sold by him to James Surget, who gave it to his daughter, Carlotta, on the occasion of her marriage to David McKittrick. Thus Elmscourt was again the property of a Surget.

The McKittrick family have lived in Elmscourt many years. They have added to the valuable collection of antique furnishings, Mrs. McKittrick bringing in superb pieces from Surget heirlooms.

An outstanding piece of Elmscourt's furnishing is a serving table, made for the Duke of Devonshire and bearing his coat-of-arms. It was a gift to Mrs. McKittrick.

In the dining room still swings the old hand-carved punka of colonial days. At every meal, a servant stands at the end of the long dining room and by rope-and-arm-power keeps the great fan (punka) gently stirring, or creating, refreshing breezes for the comfort of the diners.

The lighting of Elmscourt is the early designed candle arrangement. Over doorways, in chandeliers, sconces, and wall brackets hundreds of candles cast their welcoming, soft glow, and add undying romance to the family portrait gallery and rich rosewood furniture.

Each Spring season when tourists wend their way to Natchez for its Spring festivities, the McKittricks of Elmscourt give their famous "Ball of a Thousand Candles". Lords and Ladies, the elite of Natchez, in costume of days of long ago, greet their guests, and Elmscourt becomes today what it has been in the past, an alluring setting for colorful gatherings of notables.

THE TABLE IS A PRESENT FROM THE DUKE OF DEVONSHIRE.

THE HALL OF GLENFIELD

Glenfield

Turn to the right on the first gravel road leading from Canal street and within a stone's throw of the paved highway nestles a quaint old brick cottage surrounded by giant oaks and cedars. It is "Glenfield", the home of Mrs. Lee Field and her family.

Glenfield was built in 1812 by Charles B. Green. It is of Gothic design and is constructed of red brick and hand-hewn timbers. Like many of the old homes, "Glenfield" demonstrates two distinct types of architecture. One part is low ceilinged with brick floors, while another part has high ceilings, broad board floors, and ornate windows with heavy hand-made blinds.

Glenfield contains many rare pieces of antique furniture. A most interesting piece is an old spinning wheel, a family heirloom. It is made of hickory and is brown with age. Charred spots bear silent evidence to the old wheel's narrow escape from destruction when Indians set fire to the covered wagon bearing it while its pioneer owner was bringing his family and household goods to this section. Everything was destroyed except a few choice pieces. As one turns the wheel today it seems to hum a chant of toil, trials and tribulations.

Glenfield was originally "Glencannon", named for its former owner, William Cannon. The property is part of an original Spanish grant to John Gerault under Don Manuel Gayoso de Lemos, who was then governor of the Natchez Territory.

During the War Between the States "Glenfield" was a scene of battle, and bullet holes made in that conflict can be seen today in vivid contrast to the peace which now pervades the restful old home amid vine-covered bayous and hills.

Glenwood

Conditions at Glenwood are not conducive to pride in the hearts of Natchez people, and yet it is doubtful if any tourist leaves Natchez without hearing, in some way, about this dilapidated old place. As all things are good or bad by comparison, it may not be amiss when depicting the glory of Natchez to glimpse the other side.

A Northern tourist upon seeing Glenwood (known today as "Goat Castle") said, "Well, I don't know whether to cry or swear."

Glenwood is the home of Richard Dana, a man of aristocratic breeding and birth, and of his guardian, Miss Martha Dockery, a stalwart, dark-eyed woman who has been for many years in charge of Mr. Dana and the house.

"Dick" Dana, as he is called, and Miss Dockery are probably in their late sixties.

Dick is the son of the late Charles B. Dana, an Episcopal clergyman, and Elvira R. Dana. The Rev. Dr. Dana was from Massachusetts.

Richard was given a splendid education. He was a pianist of exceptional ability. As years passed he spent much of his fortune, living a great part of the time in the East. When he returned to Glenwood, he seemed to live the life of a hermit, living alone with his piano and his music. Gradually gray locks reached his shoulders, and long whiskers covered his face.

County officials decided it would be best to appoint a guardian for him and Miss Dockery was named. The Dana and Dockery families had been friends for generations. Miss Dockery, who was alone and growing old, was glad to accept the charge of her old friend.

A few years ago there was a murder in the neighborhood. There had been some trouble between the murdered woman and the Dockery-Dana people because of trespassing goats. The two recluses were accused of the murder. They were taken into court, held in prison, stood trial, and finally were declared "not guilty". Dana proved that at the time of the murder he was playing the piano and was not near the scene of the crime.

During the period of their incarceration, vandals ransacked "Goat Castle" and carried away many valuable relics. A guard was finally placed over the place to prevent souvenir hunters from taking the remainder of the valuable pieces. Public sympathy was aroused, and for a short time Dana and Miss Dockery were lionized. They seemed to take a new lease on life. They improved in personal appearance. They often came to town, but conditions in "Goat Castle" changed little.

Goats roam the place in undisturbed joy. Chickens roost on the foot of the great mahogany bed while Dick plays his old piano for curious tourists who pay twenty-five cents to see the old aristocrat, and Miss Dockery tells stories of the former wealth and prestige of her friend, who desired to withdraw from the world.

Glenwood is falling. Neglect and age are causing decay. The stables and out-houses are piles of mortar and decayed timbers, though the grounds are still beautiful with majestic moss-draped oaks and flowering magnolias.

GLENWOOD (known today as "Goat Castle")

Gloucester

A mile drive from the city limits of Natchez, along a roadway where moss-draped boughs overlap into a verdant shelter, brings one in view of a stately red brick mansion. It is Gloucester. Still half concealed by giant oaks and tropical growth, it seems a great ruby in a gray-gold setting.

Gloucester is surrounded by 250 acres of farm land and virgin timber. It was built about 1800, and is of solid brick construction. Huge Corinthian columns support spacious galleries across the broad front. The windows are iron barred and shuttered.

This mansion is of historic interest. It was the home of Governor Winthrop Sargent, who was the first Governor of Mississippi Territory.

Front twin doorways are an unusual feature. Inside these doors are the heavy wooden bars, the original fastenings against unfriendly Indian tribes and traveling bandits, who were not infrequent during the early days of life at Gloucester.

The twin doors open into a wide hallway which contains a graceful curving stairway leading to hall and bedrooms above.

Gloucester has a splendid library of rare first editions and valuable old books. The drawing room contains Colonial furniture and paintings by masters.

Upon the death of Governor Sargent, Gloucester became the property of his wife, who, in turn, willed it to her son, George Washington Sargent.

During the occupation of Natchez by Federal troops, the young Sargent was called to the doorway of Gloucester, and shot by two soldiers to whom he had given greeting. Stains of the life-blood of this George Washington Sargent are still visible on the doorway of Gloucester. The murdered boy was buried beside his father in the family burial ground across the road from the home.

GRAND HALLWAY OF GLOUCESTER

In the Negro quarters there are weird tales of ghosts wandering over the premises. "Two tall ghosts, in uniform, carrying guns, come on dark rainy nights when the owls hoot in the oaks above the graves."

Records show that in 1877 Gloucester was sold to James Surget, who was one of Natchez' earliest and most affluent citizens. This home was continuously owned by the Surget family for sixty years, until the recent death of Mrs. Katherine Boyd Surget, when the property was bequeathed to its present owner, Lenox Stanton.

Mr. and Mrs. Stanton hold dear every Gloucester tradition and take pride in maintaining the home and grounds in their original state of perfection.

Hawthorne

On the famous Natchez Trace Highway, within calling distance of the Lower Woodville road, through a narrow gateway flanked by giant oaks, is a quaint little cottage, "Hawthorne".

It is the old Southern Planter type home, a story-and-a-half.

A beautiful double front door with panels of early period thin glass and an exquisitely wrought fanlight above give an atmosphere of friendliness to the entrance.

Architects interested in the unusual find charm in the hand-hewn stairway which rises from the broad back hall to the rooms above.

"Hawthorne" more than a century ago belonged to a family named Overaker who sold the place with its sixty acres of wooded land to the Dunbar family, under whose regime this quaint old home sheltered and entertained the elite of the South as early as 1837. It is believed that Hawthorne was built by the Tichenor family about 1825.

For many years this old place was vacant. Lumber mills and grist mills crowded too near, but the property was recently bought by the family of William McGehee, who are reclaiming "Hawthorne". Every line of the period architecture is being followed, and "Hawthorne", its meadows and gardens, will soon be restored as in stage coach days to greet today its motor car visitors. The history of Hawthorne is a sad story with a hopeful ending.

Hope Farm

A few years ago when "Hope Farm" fell into the hands of Mr. and Mrs. Balfour Miller it was truly "getting a break" for rehabilitation. Today when one steps into this old Spanish house, built about 1775, there breathes from every crevice and corner the true atmosphere of the Old South.

The original portion of Hope Farm, its English wing, is believed to have been built by Marcus Haller. The front, the straight, low, Spanish portion, was built by the Spanish Governor, de Grand Pre, about the year 1790.

The low sweeping roof extending over a broad portico across the entire front of the house is upheld by seven hand-hewn cypress columns. Broad steps lead from the driveway to the terraced yard. This yard is a veritable bouquet of old-fashioned small flowers, bordered by boxwood and flanked by syringa, japonica, and other old-fashioned evergreen shrubs. A radiant variety of orchid-like irises dot the entire approach to the old brick steps of the terrace.

For ninety years Hope Farm belonged to the Montgomery family; of the last generation of ten children (seven girls and three boys) two of the sisters lived in spinsterhood at Hope Farm until within the last few years when the property was acquired by the Millers.

Restoration of exterior and interior has been done with exceeding care to hold every line of the original house. There were no nails in the day when Hope Farm was built and its timbers are held together by wooden pegs.

The front door leads directly into a huge living room, which opens through an archway into a large dining room. These two rooms extend across the entire front.

The welcoming gate of Hope Farm opens at the intersection of Homochitto street on the drive to Duncan Park.

Homewood

It required five years to build this palatial mansion of brick, cement, and iron grill, and until recently "Homewood", exterior and interior, was in a perfect state of preservation — just as it was the day of its completion, more than 75 years ago. Homewood was destroyed by fire, January 2, 1940.

By reason of its solid masonry (built to withstand the storms), its architectural lines, and the grace and magnificence of its iron trimmings, architects of note from all over the country came to inspect and to study "Homewood".

One million home-burned brick were used in the main structure. Copper pipes laid in cement supplied the huge cisterns throughout the years with cold drinking water. This construction represented the work of hundreds of slaves. All locks, hinges, and door knobs were of silver. The fluted Ionic columns and grill work were imported from Spain.

Approaching Homewood by the magnificent forest driveway, it was a wonderfully imposing structure with a front of thirty-foot columns, an upper balcony of cast iron grill, and massive double panel entrance doors flanked on either side by expensive ruby glass which was imported from Belgium.

There were six rooms on the ground floor, connected by huge sliding mahogany doors, making it possible to open the entire floor into one immense room, 80 feet long. Leading to six rooms and cross halls above was a fan spread stairway. The top floor was a peculiarly constructed octagonal hall surrounded by eight large closets or storage rooms with cedar linings.

The mantels in Homewood attracted much attention because of their delicate beauty and apparent value. In the drawing room the mantel was of white marble, while in the dining room stood one of pink marble with deep rose tracings.

Homewood had no historic interest but it was an outstanding example of the advanced architectural ideas of the builders of Southern ante-bellum homes. It was built for a gift from David Hunt to his daughter, Catherine, and her husband, William L. Balfour.

The most recent owners, Mr. and Mrs. Kingsly Swan, spared no expense in maintaining this magnificent home and its spacious grounds in model perfection.

Homewood was the scene of the famous double wedding so effectively described in Stark Young's *So Red the Rose*.

MAJESTIC RUINS OF HOMEWOOD

Inglewood

A Southern planter's typical home, "Inglewood" stands today as the perfection of a beautiful dream recalled from crumbling ruins of years long gone. More than a century ago this quaint old story-and-a-half house was built by Gustavus Calhoun, who practiced medicine in Natchez Territory in 1829—back in the days when calls were made on horseback and the doctor carried along his miniature drug store in his "saddle bags". Dr. Calhoun was a friend and contemporary of Dr. Stephen Duncan of "Auburn".

In 1858 "Inglewood" became the home of Edward M. Blackburn through his marriage into the Calhoun family. It has been for many years known as "the old Blackburn place." Here the last member of the Natchez Blackburn family lived until the old house was about to tumble down. Then the place was purchased by Dr. Wallace Smith, a young physician who came with his bride to reclaim and rebuild Inglewood along the exact lines of its original architectural design.

The old gardens of Inglewood were once as famous for beauty as those of "Arlington" and "Melrose" but the gardens too passed with the old families. Doctor and Mrs. Smith are replanting, and are replacing walks and borders of old-fashioned boxwood, everything to conform as nearly as possible to original design.

Inglewood, like all Natchez homes, is off the highway, secluded by forests, and only by careful observation can one glimpse the gleaming white outlines of this beautiful old plantation home.

The approach to the house is marked at the public highway by a wrought iron replica of the old-fashioned doctor's horse and buggy. Inglewood is today, as it was originally, the property of a practicing physician's family.

Jefferson College

Founded in 1802, Jefferson Military College is the oldest college for boys in the State of Mississippi, and one of the oldest in the United States.

It was here that the South's beloved Jefferson Davis, who became President of the Confederacy, attended school when he was ten years old.

After the battle of New Orleans Gen. Andrew Jackson rested his victorious army on the campus of this college, which is located six miles from the city of Natchez.

Mississippi was a territory when the college came into existence. On the spot where the constitution of the State of Mississippi was adopted is a marker commemorating the birth of Mississippi as a State. The marker was erected May 14, 1935, the 119th anniversary of the State.

Near the front gate of the college there are two giant gnarled liveoaks, known as the Aaron Burr oaks because they stood in front of the old courthouse where Aaron Burr was tried for treason against the United States. The old courthouse was demolished ages ago but the oaks stand sentinel with wide spreading boughs marking the spot famous in history and in story.

King's Tavern

In the days when Indians roamed the territory of Natchez, block houses were built by the white settlers who came that way. These were sturdy, well-fortified houses built to protect occupants against Indian outbreaks. Such is King's Tavern — an inconspicuous, faded, old wooden structure on a high brick foundation.

Although unostentatious, King's Tavern is important. According to the records it is the oldest building in this part of the South. Parts of St. Augustine, Florida, are somewhat older. Its very atmosphere breathes of days and people long dead; of Indians, of Spanish and English and French noblemen; of weary travelers over foot paths or by river boats, wandering into the old Tavern, resting, and then departing, disappearing from the face of the earth.

The house is more than 170 years old. Records show that "the first United States mail brought over the Natchez Trace was delivered to King's Tavern by an Indian runner and was distributed from this point."

The timbers are held together by wooden pegs and beams. The heavier timbers are of the type used in the construction of large ships of that period. Ceilings in the rooms are low. Doors and windows are heavy with narrow frames. The sills and sleepers of the building show the rope holes, again indicating that timbers came from old sailing vessels.

The earliest official record of transfer of this property shows 1789 as the year it was granted to Richard King, a member of the King family of Long Island, New York, and by him it was given the name "King's Tavern". Formerly it had been known as the Bledsoe House.

For a period of about 115 years the property has been owned and occupied by the descendants of Mrs. Elizabeth Postlethwaite.

An interesting relic of bygone years is a portrait in oils of the late Samuel Postlethwaite III, who was Mayor of Natchez in 1825 when the great Lafayette visited the little village. This portrait is signed by the artist, Benjamin West.

Mrs. A. C. Register and Mrs. Jean Register Modsett, descendants of the Postlethwaite family, are the present owners and occupants of King's Tavern.

Legend:

> At night, when all's dark and quiet at King's Tavern, ghosts of Indian warriors, in full dress of their native tribe, wander through the old Tap Room, loll and lean against the old bar, peer out through small crevices, and then disappear through the heavy doors which lead onto the street.

MAIN DOOR AT KING'S TAVERN WHERE INDIAN RUNNERS LEFT THE MAIL

Bullet holes in the door are from an Indian attack during the early days of Natchez.

Lansdown

Lansdown has been the home of the Marshall family for more than eighty-five years. Like many other magnificent plantation homes around Natchez, Lansdown was a wedding gift to Mr. and Mrs. George Marshall, whose descendants of the same name own and occupy today this comfortable Georgian type house.

Lansdown is an unpretentious but quite substantial structure with a broad front portico enclosed by artistic grill bannisters fashioned in Greek pattern. Broad, spreading steps lead down to a brick walk, and on each side stand the old carriage blocks of yesteryear.

Portraits by famous artists of earlier generations of Marshalls, including a portrait of Levin R. Marshall by Sully, look down on gorgeous rosewood and mahogany furnishings of their own selection placed in Lansdown.

The china and silver in this home are the pride of the present generation of Marshalls. Much of the original china is in use today. Many pieces of the original Robert E. Lee furnishings of "Stratford Hall" are now in Lansdown. Within the past few months the younger generation at Lansdown discovered several pieces of silver bearing the unmistakable mark of Robert E. Lee.

Lansdown came to the Marshalls through Mrs. Charlotte Hunt Marshall. Natchez had a great benefactor in David Hunt, the father of Charlotte Hunt Marshall. It was he who made possible the Chamberlain-Hunt Military Academy at Port Gibson, Mississippi, one of the first schools for boys in the Southland. It is still an excellent school for young men.

Today Lansdown is owned and occupied by George Marshall III and Mrs. Agnes Marshall Ward, lineal descendants of the original owner, who named the place "Lansdown" by virtue of his friendship for the celebrated Marquis of Lansdown, England.

Linden

The origin of Linden seems lost to history although it is known to have existed as early as 1790. It came to ancestors of the present owners a hundred years ago, and has been owned and occupied by the A. M. Feltus family for several generations.

Nature seems to exert herself to give to Linden a perfect setting. Surrounding the magnificently constructed house, with its 98 feet of gallery, are dozens of oak trees, draped in long gray moss which sweeps the very eaves of the dwelling. Standing in the artistic entrance of Linden one sees the outside world through growing draperies of swaying gray lace.

The architecture of Linden is as unusual as it is simple. The center portion is two stories, flanked on each side by single-storied rooms. A gallery runs the entire width of the building. To the rear of the single-storied rooms is a long two-storied wing. Each wing is a complete apartment.

The furnishings are rare and exquisite, producing a feeling of restfulness and satisfaction. "Linden" has three paintings by Audubon, and an interesting portrait of the song-bird, Jenny Lind.

The driveway through the grounds of Linden leads past the front entrance entirely around the house and passes its beautifully kept gardens. A circle driveway which leads out through the bricked entrance affords a final glimpse of the stately white house in the distance, not unlike "Mount Vernon". The view across the hill brings "Monmouth", a neighboring mansion, to the eye as another delightful prospect.

LINDEN — Dining Room With Punka

Greenleaves

"Greenleaves", built prior to 1812, is a town house — a great rambling cottage type of architecture in the very heart of Natchez. It is as sturdy as the old gnarled oaks which seem to hold it in their protecting boughs. It represents comfort, luxury, and beauty without ostentation or pretense.

The halls and rooms are palatial in size and appointments. The house as originally constructed shows that it was built to endure. It was remodeled in the early 40's by the grandfather of the present owners.

A wealth of the original furnishings in solid mahogany and rosewood and many rare museum pieces have remained in Greenleaves throughout generations, and are today as beautiful as the day they came from foreign shores.

The present owners, Mr. and Mrs. Melchoir Beltzhoover, the third generation of the Koontz family to occupy Greenleaves, grace this ante-bellum home with pardonable pride of possession.

The family of the original owners of Greenleaves was wiped out during a yellow fever epidemic, the entire family filling one grave. Eventually Greenleaves was bought by George Washington Koontz of Pennsylvania, who became a leading influence, financially and socially, in Natchez. Children of the present occupants of Greenleaves are the fourth generation of the Koontz family to enjoy this luxurious home.

Mr. Beltzhoover's ownership of this property is shared with his sister, Mrs. Guy Robinson, who is a resident of New York state.

Legend:

> Under the giant livecoaks at the rear of Greenleaves the Natchez tribe of Indians held their annual pow-wows and decided all momentous questions.

Longwood

Longwood stands in a moss-tangled forest. It is a monument to a dream that was interrupted by the tragedy of the War Between the States in 1861-'65. It was to have been a gorgeous structure of Moorish design, planned by Sloan of Philadelphia, who in those days had no equal as artist-architect.

Longwood was being built for Dr. Haller Nutt. Landscape gardeners came from abroad, and even today rare imported shrubs and trees form a part of the dense growth around the unfinished gardens.

When the house reached its present point of construction, with more than a hundred thousand dollars already invested, there came the cry of war and the call to arms. Workmen laid down their tools and took their guns and never returned to the task of completing Longwood.

The deep concrete foundation, the outside framework, and some of the trimmings of the house were well under way. Today there are huge sections of carved moulding, old paint buckets and brushes, tool boxes, and carpenter's implements scattered about the upper floors — just as they were left almost 75 years ago.

The house, begun in the late 50's, is of brick, burned by slaves on the place, with columns and grill work of hand-carved, time-enduring cypress. The ground floor contained a nursery and an adjoining apartment for a white housekeeper and governess, a card room, a billiard room, wine cellar, and heating plant. This floor is the only part of the building that reached anything like completion. The upper floors were boarded up. All orders for materials, marble stairway, mosaic floors, and elaborate furnishings were canceled. Many of these orders had been placed in Italy and France. Some costly pieces were en route on the high seas. A few items were returned and others are now in national museums.

Dr. Nutt died in 1864, survived by his wife and a large family of children. One of the descendants of these children now occupies the finished lower floor or basement of Longwood. There is on this floor a huge rotunda and eight large rooms, surrounded by a moat. Many relics of past generations adorn these quarters, including antiques from different branches of the family.

There are several pieces of richly carved rosewood furniture, an exquisite old grand piano, and oil portraits of Dr. Nutt and his beautiful blonde wife by famous old-world artists.

James and Merritt Ward of Natchez and Mrs. Julia Ward Blanchard of New York City are the present owners of Longwood.

Planned as a palatial home for a family of eleven children and eight hundred slaves, today Longwood (often referred to as "Nutt's Folly") is occupied by Merritt Ward and one servant.

LONGWOOD — "NUTT'S FOLLY"

Magnolia Vale

A few hundred feet below the city of Natchez, along the river edge, is an extension of land on which the first Natchez was situated. This old town was known as "Natchez Under the Hill". The commercial center of the old Natchez has passed into decay. The buildings that sheltered the river men, the gambling "joints" that housed the riff-raff of those steamboat days, have long since tumbled into the river. Driving down a long and steep shelf of land, at the north end of what was old Natchez, one comes to the gate of a castle-like home in the heart of a garden which is always beautiful with blossoms. It is "Magnolia Vale".

This house was built about 110 years ago by Andrew Brown and is owned today by Andrew B. Learned, a direct descendant.

Andrew Brown was a native of Scotland, and a great lover of flowers. After building a home of the early American type, with wide galleries, handsome Doric columns, spacious halls and large rooms, he found self-expression in creating a garden which has been famous for generations, from St. Louis to New Orleans, as "Brown's Gardens".

A formal driveway, bordered with Louis Philippe roses, leads to the mansion. Giant magnolias and evergreen laurimundi splash the landscape with white and green. Formal flower beds, with boxwood borders, cover the entire acreage of the foreground to Magnolia Vale.

The Mississippi River has continuously eaten into the grounds of Magnolia Vale until much of this promontory has vanished into the waters. Although the great house shows marked evidence of "settling" from year to year, and is occupied now by a caretaker only, the gardens are given constant attention. The same trim boxwood hedges, the same formal walks and beloved flower beds, the same shrubs, the same tall trees, and the maze of gardenia and japonica greet the visitor and shed perfume across the broad and mighty river, which ravenously eats at the very roots of these gorgeous plants.

Mount Repose

Here is a huge, comfortable, old-fashioned, country gentleman's home — in appearance and in literal fact "Mount Repose". The name aptly describes the first impression of every visitor.

The house is situated on an elevation, surrounded by broad green acres.

Built in the early 1800's, Mount Repose has been the scene of much that is interesting in the story of Natchez. It is part of the original estate of William Bisland, a Scotsman. From this family comes the author Elizabeth Bisland who through close association with Lafcadio Hearn, when both of them worked for the old New Orleans *Picayune,* was able to write the interesting life of that genius. This book and many others by Elizabeth Bisland, including *Candle of Understanding* and *The Case of John Smith,* can be found in public libraries today.

The present owners of Mount Repose, Mr. and Mrs. A. R. Baldwin of New York, are direct descendants of the Bisland family. Its present occupants, the J. D. Shields family are also descendants of the Bislands. Mrs. Shields is a descendant of the renowned English beauty, Margaret Watts, who married the Spanish Governor, Manuel Gayoso de Lemos, who is prominently identified with Natchez' earliest history.

The original furnishings of Mount Repose have gone out to Bisland heirs, and yet valuable antiques and family portraits remain in the old house.

An interesting story is told of a wager expressive of the loyalty of William Bisland to Henry Clay.

Mr. Bisland believed that Henry Clay should be, and would be, the next president of the United States. He laid a wager in accordance with his belief. He had just planted a formal line of sentinel trees along a driveway to the main entrance of Mount Repose. He openly declared that this driveway would be closed until Clay was elected. He then proceeded with great preparations for its formal opening, but history tells why today there grow two long lines of well-spaced trees from the big front gate to the house — that gate unopened through the years! The entrance to Mount Repose is through the side gate. Henry Clay was never elected president.

Melmont

'Way back in 1839, when Henry Basil Shaw married Mary Elizabeth Lattimore, profound consideration was given to naming the homes and estates of Natchez. It is almost certain that the mistress of Melmont pondered long and consulted her family before deciding the name. She chose to use the three initials of Mary Elizabeth Lattimore to form the first part of the name, "Mel", and added "mont" because the mansion stood mounted on a rolling acreage. Thus "Melmont" was coined.

Melmont is unlike other Natchez homes. The architecture is its own peculiar type. A sturdy, well-built house, it has for almost a century cared for Natchez' foremost citizens and their illustrious guests. Claiborne, the historian, Judge Samuel Brooks, and other prominent men spent much time at Melmont.

The acreage around Melmont has been sold and modern homes have been built on the land. Melmont is now a palatial town house, no longer a country home.

Melmont was within the Federal lines during the War Between the States. When Natchez was shelled from the river in 1862 shells fell in the yard and gardens and destroyed giant oak trees and landscaping.

The interior decoration and furnishing are to a great extent from the original family although many handsome pieces have been added by subsequent owners. Mrs. John Ayres and her sister, Miss Corinne Henderson, have occupied this home for many years. Mrs. Ayers especially prizes a mahogany bureau which has chests on either side for storing wigs.

MELMONT — Drawing Room

A valuable Hepplewhite desk in the drawing room attracts much interest. It belonged to the renowned John Henderson, and it was here he is believed to have written an appeal to Congress in 1798 "for schools for the education of children and provision for regular ministry of the Gospel."

Melmont is well preserved, exterior and interior, and holds great charm for all who come within its portals.

MELROSE

POND ON DRIVEWAY TO THE HOUSE

(*opposite*) THE DRAWING ROOM. The old-fashioned "courting set" had a center seat for the chaperon, who was ever present during boy and girl visits.

Melrose

Melrose, called "the perfect ante-bellum home", is located about a mile from Natchez city limits. This model mansion, built in the early 40's, owned and occupied by Mr. and Mrs. George M. D. Kelly, is, by courtesy of the owners, opened for inspection during the annual Pilgrimage celebration of the Natchez Garden Club. In an entire day one can only glimpse Melrose and its treasures. Another full day could be well spent in the surrounding woodlands and boxwood bordered gardens.

Built in 1845 by Judge Edward Turner for his daughter, Mrs. McMurran, it was purchased immediately after the War Between the States by George Malin Davis, grandfather of the present owner, George Malin Davis Kelly. Mr. Kelly has with great pride of possession kept the Melrose home and estate in its original perfection.

PUNKA OVER DINING ROOM TABLE

The approach to Melrose is through acres of lawn as smooth as stretched velvet. The house is an imposing brick building of the square Georgian architectural design, with upper and lower porticos, and supporting Ionic columns.

The front door is of attractive Colonial style with diamond shaped sidelights. A broad sweep of steps lead to the wide portico.

A spacious hall runs through the lower floor. It is appropriately furnished in rare old pieces; among these is an unusual table which is set with semi-precious stones, and an ancient grandfather's clock. The lighting for this grand hallway is provided by numerous rows of candles, held in dainty but substantial frames. The floor covering (which is the original) attracts immediate attention by reason of its beauty, unique design, and quality. It can be best described as a striking inlay of unknown origin.

To the right of the hall is the front drawing room. The rosewood furniture is Empire style, and is in as perfect condition today as on the day of its purchase.

74

TPYICAL BEDROOM PIECES — MELROSE

To the left is a dining room 20 feet square. Black marble mantels add dignity to the room. A handsome mahogany punka swings over the dining table. This bespeaks undeniable antiquity. Until quite recently the owners of Melrose cared for several old slaves who pulled the punka to create breezes for the comfort of the family during meals.

Melrose still uses its outside brick kitchen, reached by a broad brick walk from the main house. Above the kitchen are quarters for the house servants.

The upper floors of Melrose contain bedrooms, halls, and a sewing room. Massive beds so high that occupants must climb in by a set of specially made mahogany steps; heavy bureaus, armoirs, dressing tables, tilt top tables, and day bed—all are heirlooms of the original owners and of the present owners.

Mr. Davis (the grandfather of the present owner) came South from Pennsylvania many years before the war of '61, and was educated at Sewanee College, Sewanee, Tennessee. His only daughter married Dr. Stephen Kelly of New York, and that daughter became the mother of George M. D. Kelly, the present owner of Melrose mansion.

George M. D. Kelly and his wife, who was Miss Ethel Moore, are members of old New York families but have long since adopted the Southland as their home.

Monmouth

Near "Linden", on a velvety lawn guarded by great oaks, stands a Grecian-type mansion. This is Monmouth, now owned and maintained by Mrs. Hubert Barnum. Mrs. Barnum, owner of "Arlington", the adjoining estate, is probably the only Natchezian who owns and operates two great ante-bellum homes.

Historically Monmouth is known as the home of John A. Quitman and his wife, Eliza. General Quitman, a hero of national renown, raised the first American flag in Mexico. He purchased this mansion and fifteen surrounding acres about the year 1826.

Edith Wyatt Moore in her story of Monmouth says: "John A. Quitman and Eliza Turner drew a marriage contract prior to their wedding. He relinquished all right of inheritance to her property in case of her death without children. He gave her the right to handle slaves and property or dispose of same without his consent." General Quitman was a native of New York.

A man of great popularity and military distinction, General Quitman's home became the scene of many gatherings of the notables of America. Monmouth was classed among the most perfectly appointed homes of its day.

General Quitman died in 1859 from what was suspected as the effect of slow poison administered at a banquet given in honor of President Buchanan.

For a period following General Quitman's death his beloved Monmouth was vacant. It became dilapidated from disuse, and after passing through many hands was purchased by Mrs. Annie Gwynne, who is now Mrs. Barnum. Every part has been repaired or renewed and the old mansion stands today in majestic perfection.

Great square pillars support the upper portico, which is encircled by attractive lattice grill work. The walls are of brick. The doors, with fan transoms and side-lights, and the window frames are made of hand-carved wood. Spacious halls, huge rooms with high ceilings, and a pervading air of solid, substantial structure make Monmouth a monument eternal to a man whose memory shall never die — a man of whom it was said, "He is Mississippi's best-loved citizen."

The original furnishings of Monmouth are long since gone. These were supplanted by rare antiques from the superb collection of Mrs. Barnum's family, the Greens, who founded Greensboro, North Carolina.

MILK HOUSE AND SERVANTS' QUARTERS — MONMOUTH

Monteigne

"Monteigne" is a recently acquired possession of one of Natchez' most valued families, Mrs. Mary Worrell Kendall and Mr. and Mrs. William Kendall. It was built in 1855 as the home of Gen. William T. Martin of the Confederacy, whose features are carved on Stone Mountain as a representative of the State of Mississippi. Hand-hewn timbers discovered when excavating the foundation for "Monteigne" lead to the belief that this was the site of a home destroyed during the Indian Massacre of 1729.

The place bears the French Huguenot name for Martin, "Monteigne". It is unlike any of the old homes around Natchez. Predominantly Georgian in appearance, Monteigne stands out distinctively. A solid, two-story structure, built of sturdiest timbers, this home has withstood the ravages of time and the desecration of opposing forces during the War Between the States.

It is said that horses were "stalled" in the parlors by Yankee soldiers, rosewood furniture used for kindling fires, and valuable silver and brass melted and lost.

MONTEIGNE — PATIO

Upon his return from the war, General Martin saw the destruction of the beauty of his house and its grounds. With the undismayed courage of a great man who knows how to overcome defeat, he began the restoration of his home and its eleven acres of yard and gardens.

When Leslie Carpenter bought Monteigne in 1928 Natchez was assured another perfect estate. Terraced lawns and rose gardens were brought to life; driveways, trellises, shrubbery, and flagged walks were restored to this classic home.

The interior of Monteigne is stately — formal and yet inviting — with the black and white mosaic floor in its great entrance hall.

Monteigne recently passed from the Carpenters to the present owners, Mrs. Mary Worrell Kendall, her son, William, and his wife and their two little daughters.

ROSE GARDEN   MONTEIGNE   LILY POOL

Myrtle Terrace

Substantial and compact, this Colonial cottage is one of the reclaimed small ante-bellum homes of Natchez. Built in the 1830's, it is more than a century old.

In 1844 Myrtle Terrace was purchased by the late L. N. Carpenter, who, in turn, sold it to the renowned Captain Thomas Leathers of steamboat fame. The agreement to buy stipulated in minute detail that the property must be put in "ship shape", carefully specifying "hinges on the windows, fastenings on the cellar door, latches on the gates, blinds on all windows except the dormers, building a stable and a carriage house".

Captain Leathers was identified with the famous *Natchez-Robert E. Lee* steamboat race from New Orleans to St. Louis, on the Mississippi river, in 1870. The prize was $20,000. The race has become an epic. So thrilling is it in the history of river traffic it was dramatized in a recent celebration on the Pacific Coast.

Captain Leathers of the *Natchez* lost the race to Captain Cannon of the *Robert E. Lee* not because he had a slower boat but because of his over-confidence. He traveled nonchalantly and made all his regular stops. In the pinch he would not jeopardize the safety of his passengers by pressing his boilers beyond the safety point.

Captain Leathers lived in Myrtle Terrace for many years, and the place is still known as the "home of the Captain of the steamboat *Natchez*". It is now owned and occupied by Mr. and Mrs. Dan Tucker, who have reclaimed the old lines of the house and have added modern interior improvements.

Propinquity

In the long ago, when each Southern plantation was identified by a specially chosen name, the naming of homes around Natchez was a great event. When land was opened and a home built, a recorded name was given, and neither time nor change of owner or occupant changed the name of that plantation. Interesting indeed are the stories of the names selected.

"Propinquity" was named in 1810 by its owner, Brigadier General Leonard Covington, and was so named because its lands adjoined Fort Dearborn where he was in command of a troop of Light Dragoons. Today Propinquity is appropriate as "near to nature".

The plantation belonged originally to one William Belk. The records show that in 1797 a committee met at this place for the purpose of appointing a Public Safety organization, the first American political assembly held in the Lower Mississippi Valley.

For several generations Propinquity has been owned by the descendants of Jane Long, the famous "Mother of Texas", who spent many happy days in this quaint old home. It is still a reliquary for interesting possessions of the Texas heroine.

Situated on a side road off the original "Natchez Trace", this old house is built on simple early American lines. A wide center hall with a deep mahogany stairway runs the length of the two huge rooms on either side. Green shuttered, small pane windows, a solid three-panel front door with straight glass sidelights, and a small upper and lower portico complete the simple picture of this old home.

The furnishings are of the original purchase. There is a tiny melodeon in the parlor. Its quaint type indicates very early "vintage" — a rare museum piece.

PROPINQUITY

SPINET

HAND MADE WAX FRUIT
UNDER A GLASS GLOBE

Bedrooms where rested the nobility of the land in earlier days are still prim and precise with poster beds in their original draperies, mahogany armoirs, bureaus with numerous side compartments and many mirrors to please the fancy of milady of the early fifties.

In the dining room there is an exquisite set of china, and despite the fact that it has been in daily use for more than one hundred years, only two small pieces are missing from the set of 200 pieces. This gives an idea of the order and system, and the appreciation for the valuable and beautiful at Propinquity.

The house is occupied by Miss Rebecca Miller and Mrs. M. E. Fauntleroy, who are descendants of the renowned Jane Long.

RAVENNA *(front)*

AZALEAS,
LITTLE RAVENNA

84

Ravenna

At the end of Union street, on ten acres of ground which edges a great ravine or bayou, stands Ravenna, the present home of Mrs. Richard I. Metcalf.

Ravenna was built more than one hundred years ago by the Harris family. It has stood the test of time and of the tornado of 1840. It stands today in the superior dignity of perfection. The property was acquired by the family of its present owner about eighty years ago.

Ravenna shows every evidence of an inherited love of flowers. This comes from Andrew Brown of "Brown's Gardens", and Mrs. Metcalf, a direct descendant, has expressed that inherited taste and talent in the beautification of Ravenna.

The house is the large Colonial type. An outstanding feature of the interior is an exquisite stairway and a great assembly of unusual, massive antiques.

The charm of Ravenna is its setting. Facing a great ravine, the old home is surrounded by flowers. A huge wisteria vine covers the front of the house with purple blossoms. The side of the place toward the town is enclosed by a high iron fence of massive design. The main entrance is through heavy iron gates that lead along the winding tulip bordered driveway to the front portico. Bordering this driveway are radiant azalea bushes and japonicas, while at certain seasons of the year the deep pink of flowering peach trees and almond trees give vivid color splotches which intensify the beauty of these grounds.

A point of interesting antiquity at Ravenna is the name "Caroline Harris" scratched with a diamond into a window pane. This proves conclusively that the windows were there in 1840 when the Harrises owned Ravenna.

During the War Between the States the peace of Ravenna was greatly disturbed by Federal soldiers who ordered the Metcalfs to leave this home. Mrs. Metcalf was suspected of communicating with the Confederate soldiers through the bayou.

After the war Ravenna was reclaimed and again occupied by the Metcalf family.

"Little Ravenna", the cottage home of the late Mrs. Zulika Metcalf Lawrence, stands on the Ravenna grounds, as does also a palatial residence occupied by Mrs. Roan Fleming Byrnes, who is a leading spirit in promoting the great Natchez Trace highway project.

This group of family homes, under the sheltering eaves of the parent home, Ravenna, eloquently bespeaks that close and lovable family life of the South as it has existed for generations.

The lyre motif in mirror and table
is unusual. Tester bed is typical.

Queen of a recent
Confederate Ball,
Miss Roane Adams,
poses beneath the
portrait of her
grandmother in the
drawing room of Ravenna.

Oakland

Among the numerous ante-bellum homes of Natchez which are today owned and occupied by lineal descendants of the original owners "Oakland" stands preeminent. Built in 1838 for Catherine Chotard Eustis, the granddaughter of Major Stephen Minor, this home remains in the possession of the Minor family. The present owner is Mrs. Jeanne Minor McDowell. Major Minor was the last Governor of the Natchez District under Spanish rule.

Oakland is located in secluded grounds, and, as its name implies, stands in a land of oaks.

The house is a substantial brick building with a wide front portico and broad brick steps. The spacious center hallway opens with heavy mahogany entrance doors into an old-fashioned parlor on the right and a large dining room on the left. The walls are covered with the original paper.

Many pieces of the original furnishings remain. Several rare pieces were brought to Oakland from "Concord", which was the Governor's official mansion and was destroyed by fire.

The Minors were lovers of race horses, and valuable paintings of beautiful horses owned by the family adorn the walls. Two especially fine horse pictures are by Troye. Many silver trophies of racing victories form an interesting part of Oakland possessions.

In this house is a bed of unique type, known as "a family bed". It is a huge four-poster with silken tester. As broad as it is long, there is plenty of room for six persons to sleep comfortably!

Ante-bellum gardens wherein grow verbena, gardenia, and sweet olive, with clipped boxwood borders, complete the handsome setting of Oakland.

Richmond

Life at Richmond today seems a continuous house party. The present owners (seven daughters, one son, and one granddaughter of the late Shelby Marshall) are the fifth and sixth generations of the illustrious Levin R. Marshall family to own and occupy this old and hospitable mansion. It contains 41 rooms.

The architecture of Richmond shows three distinct styles. The original center building, 153 years old, is of Spanish design; the front, 105 years old, is of Greek design; and 77 years ago the square English portion of the house was built.

The Spanish part, constructed of sturdy hand-hewn timbers, brick, and cement, is in an excellent state of preservation. It has stood without reconstruction throughout the years. There is a cement patio on the ground level, and cypress steps with artistic iron grill rails reach the main floor from the outside. Here one can sound the door knocker, and soon hear heavy wooden bars being lifted. This was the security against Indians and other intruders of early days, and such protection remains intact at Richmond.

In 1832 Richmond became the property of Levin R. Marshall, great-great-grandfather of the present owners, and it was he who added the lovely Greek portion. This addition contains six large rooms on the main floor and four in the basement.

Twenty-eight years later, in order to accommodate a rapidly growing family and numbers of guests, the red brick English addition was built in the rear.

The main entrance has a front portion with classic Corinthian columns supporting the roof. A broad hall, the length of two twenty-foot rooms, runs through the center to a formal dining room. This formal room opens with four tall folding doors into a smaller family dining room. There are double drawing rooms on the left side of the great hall.

The massive old furniture remains today in Richmond, as does the family silver, which is the most ornate and beautiful silver service in the entire South.

The front drawing room harbors a greatly prized relic of the past — the quaint concert grand piano which was used to accompany the famous song-bird Jenny Lind when, under the management of that superb showman, P. T. Barnum, she toured the South. A beautiful portrait of Jenny Lind hangs near the old piano.

Richmond contains a rich treasure store of old laces, quaint costumes, and queer candelabra. Quite recently there was discovered an assortment of pans and plumber's equipment. When assembled this "find" proved to be a bathtub of probably the 1850 model. The fastidious bather stood in a tin basin, pulled a curtain for privacy, while a slave by means of a small hand pump pumped water from a two-gallon tank overhead; this water ran over the bather, down into the basin, and was, in turn, pumped up and the bather reshowered.

Fortunes have been made and lost by Richmond owners. The generosity of Levin R. Marshall extended to the State of Texas and the town of Marshall, in Texas, is named in honor of this family.

Three of the cultures that have contributed to the charm of Natchez are
represented in Richmond. Post-Colonial Neo-Greek is shown at the left,
Spanish in the center, and English Georgian on the right.

FORT ROSALIE
Built by the French
in the early 18th
century, it was the
scene of the Indian
massacre of 1729.

Rosalie

In the Natchez country "Rosalie" is a magic name. It conjures up memories of startling days that were, and stimulates the imagination to see Indians and soldiers and people from foreign lands.

The home, "Rosalie", bears the name and is situated near the site of Fort Rosalie, which was built by the French in the early 1700's.

No home in Natchez is of greater historical importance than Rosalie. The building was started about 1820 by Peter B. Little, and required seven years for completion. All materials are of the choicest selection. Home-burned bricks and hand-hewn timbers were used in its construction.

Rosalie is situated 200 feet above the Mississippi River. It is now the home of Miss Rebecca Rumble and Mrs. James Marsh. It contains many original pieces of furniture, carpets, and exquisite chandeliers. A valuable piece is the mahogany table at which Jefferson Davis, president of the Confederacy, and U. S. Grant dined.

Mr. Little married his thirteen-year-old ward, and sent her to Baltimore to be educated. It was while she was in school that he built this mansion in which to receive her when she returned.

It is believed that the ground immediately back of Rosalie is the site of the great Indian massacre of the French in 1729.

Railroad tracks and driveways have cut through the acres that were originally Rosalie private grounds, but the yard and gardens of the old home are well kept and are filled with old-fashioned flowers and shrubbery of days long gone.

Rosalie was General Grant's headquarters during the Federal occupation of Natchez in the War Between the States.

The present occupants display with much pride the huge four-poster mahogany bed in which General Grant slept during his stay at this old house.

Rosalie has been purchased by the Daughters of the American Revolution, and will be maintained as a public shrine. Many of the encroaching industrial buildings will soon give way to the original acreage that formed the gardens of Rosalie.

THIS BED IN ROSALIE HAS A PRAYER PAD AT ITS SIDE.

Parsonage

Under the very eaves of old "Rosalie" with its historic background of Fort Rosalie, stands a sturdy square structure known as "The Parsonage".

It is a brick building with an English basement, the entrance leading by broad steps to the elevated first floor.

While of no particular historic interest, The Parsonage has its story.

It was built by Peter Little, the owner and builder of Rosalie, and bears the same evidence of sturdy construction exemplified in the larger home.

Like most men, Mr. Little wanted the privacy of his own home, while Mrs. Little, due to religious enthusiasm, felt called upon to entertain every preacher and his family who passed that way. By reason of this devotion to religious duty, "Rosalie" was kept filled with ministerial guests.

Following a long siege of such guests Mr. Little declared to his wife, "I am going to build a home for your church friends and their families". True to this decision he built a lovely home, and in November 1850 deeded it to the Methodist Church and called it "The Parsonage".

After the death of his young wife Mr. Little lived on at Rosalie, a broken-hearted, lonely old man, until, tradition tells, while ill and alone, in the dark hours of night, the master of Rosalie and builder of The Parsonage which he designed to insure his seclusion, was murdered by one of his own slaves.

Later The Parsonage was sold. Today, with its exquisite antique furnishings, it is the property of the Orrick Metcalfs, who are descendants of one of Natchez' oldest and most respected families.

Stanton Hall

In the heart of the city of Natchez stands an imposing mansion, "Stanton Hall". It is surrounded by a half-acre of rolling lawn which is enclosed by an iron fence. This strong iron fence is in a delicate design and is itself worth a small fortune.

Stanton Hall is the most handsome old home, and probably the most expensive, in the entire Natchez area. It is not of great historical value but it well represents the architectural grandeur of the Old South.

It was built during the 1851-56 period. As the building materials were imported, the house required several years for its construction.

On the first floor there are four tremendous rooms and a broad hall. Hand carvings for doors and windows, Carrara marble mantels, silver and bronze hinges, bronze chandeliers, and exquisite over-size mirrors required a specially chartered ship for their delivery to complete this handsome home. It was built for Frederick Stanton of Belfast, Ireland, and his young wife, Hulda Helm Stanton, a lady of the Natchez neighborhood.

The spacious grounds resemble a well-kept park. Aged oaks spread their moss-draped boughs in a latticed shield, as it were, across the front where white Corinthian columns support the massive portico which is outlined by iron grill railings of intricate lacy pattern.

To the right of the entrance is a large drawing room, and back of this, through an elaborate archway, is a very unusual music room. This room is decorated with murals of musical instruments on which appear the names of the great old music masters.

Woodwork and doors on the first floor are of solid mahogany, with silver hinges and silver door knobs.

After Stanton Hall passed from the original owners in the year 1894, it was used as a select school, known as "Stanton College for Young Ladies".

In August 1920 Robert T. Clarke bought Stanton Hall and has occupied it since that date. He recently sold the property to the Pilgrimage Garden Club.

Weymouth Hall

Unusual and peculiar is the construction of Weymouth Hall. It was purchased by Col. John Weymouth in 1821 and was rebuilt in 1852 by the Bullock family. It is a three-story brick building overlooking the Mississippi River, and has for its back view acres of Natchez cemetery.

The upper stories are reached by a winding stairway. The third floor is a ballroom. During the War Between the States this room was used as headquarters for Union soldiers because it gave a perfect view of the river and surrounding country.

Stark Young in *So Red the Rose* refers to Weymouth Hall and the death of Mrs. John Weymouth in the room below the Union headquarters. He gives a vivid description of the agony of the family as they watched a loved one slip away forever amid the hostile booming of drums above her bedroom.

The furnishings, woodwork, and mantels in Weymouth Hall are fascinating in perfection and antiquity. In the living room on the second floor is a black marble mantel inlaid with colored roses of mother of pearl. Fabulous offers have been declined for this mantel. There is probably not another like it in the entire South.

This old home is now owned and occupied by the Zurhellen and Morton families, who are lineal descendants of Mrs. John Weymouth.

Ruins of Windsor

Twenty-two stone Corinthian columns stand today as remnants of a grand example of ante-bellum Greek Revival architecture.

Windsor was built in 1861 by S. C. Daniel, a wealthy Mississippi planter who also had large land holdings in Louisiana. It had five stories, topped by an observatory. It is said that Mark Twain, when a Mississippi steamboat pilot, charted his course at this point by the lofty tower of Windsor.

The house and its furnishings were destroyed by fire in 1890.

Windy Hill Manor

Nine miles from Natchez, on the Liberty road, in a picturesque, moss-draped grove, stands "Windy Hill Manor", home of the Misses Stanton.

The records show that Windy Hill originally belonged to Joseph Ford. It was under the ownership of Benjamin Osmun, a close friend of Aaron Burr, that the place received its great historical interest.

After Aaron Burr had been accused of treason against his own country and released on $5,000 bail, he was invited to be the guest of his old friend Benjamin Osmun at Windy Hill.

One hundred and twenty years ago Benjamin Osmun sold this plantation to General Brandon, great-grandfather of the Stanton sisters who now occupy it. The Stantons gave the property the name of "Windy Hill Manor".

Architecturally this house, like many of the cottage type ante-bellum homes, is a surprise, when upon entering it is found to be of commodious proportions.

It is a story-and-a-half, plantation type home, with wide porch and large columns across the front.

There is a beautiful spiral stairway in the wide front hall. To the left is a large drawing room containing numerous relics of days long gone; portraits of past generations; antique furniture, and a most interesting collection of Indian relics. Also, an unusual fireplace and mantel are in this room.

Time has marched on but Windy Hill Manor remains a living, vibrant picture of the days of the ease and graciousness of the Old South. The Misses Stanton complete the perfection of this period picture.

Here our visit to the old estates comes to an end. Lack of space has prevented inclusion of all of the ante-bellum homes, but we hope that we have nevertheless captured the charm of Natchez.